Live Mindfully
52 Ways

by **Francine Marks-Weinstein, LMHC**
designed by **Sheila Weinstein**

To the best Mom, aka Grandi,
My devoted husband, Brett,
My dynamic daughters,
Sydney and Kennedy,
who all fill my heart.

Introduction

Welcome to a simple way to be mindful during your daily and weekly mundane tasks. Since I am not an avid reader, I wrote the type of book that I would like—one that is straightforward with information that is easy to practice. This book is not intended to be read cover to cover. You can flip to any page, read the exercise, and decide if you would like to practice the task mindfully.

The purpose of **Live Mindfully 52 Ways** is to guide you toward a more mindful way of life; to help you live in the moment instead of with feelings of "would have or could have" or worry about the future, with feelings of "what if" but to assist you in minimizing any symptoms of anxiety by using your senses.

My intent is for you to practice one of the 52 mindful tasks each week. Of course, you may practice at your own pace and repeat tasks as often as you like. As you read each entry, you will notice a running theme.

Each entry was created to help you perform a task mindfully by incorporating your senses—what is in your visual field, what you hear, what you smell, what you taste, and what you feel. By incorporating all your senses, you learn to be fully engaged with yourself.

Mindfulness means being present in your moment. According to many studies, a mindfulness practice can help reduce anxiety and stress along with decreasing depressive symptoms. It can increase emotional regulation, which can result in an efficient way to improve wellness and the quality of your life.

This unique look at mindfulness teaches you how to refocus behaviors in order to have a different mindset to carry out some of the most mundane daily/weekly tasks. My advice to you is to start now. There's no need to wait. Take it one task at a time to practice being present in your moment. You can and you will live more mindfully until it becomes a part of your daily life.

You got this!

About The Author

Francine Marks-Weinstein is a licensed mental health counselor in Florida and earned a master's degree in general clinical psychology from the University of Houston-Clear Lake. Francine specializes in mindfulness cognitive behavioral psychotherapy. She has been in private practice for over twenty-five years, working with adults, couples, children, LGTBQ+, and seniors. Francine struggled with symptoms of anxiety her whole life until she learned how to become present with her own thoughts and behaviors. Practicing mindfulness as a way of life has helped alleviate her own anxious behavior. Francine married her high-school sweetheart, Brett, and is a proud mother of two daughters, Sydney and Kennedy.

Whether it is sunscreen, makeup, or moisturizer, **apply facial products mindfully**. Make looking in the mirror your mindful moment each day. As your beautiful reflection gazes back at you, observe the structure of your face and the shape of your nose and lips. Notice your skin and eye color. You may choose to listen intently to your positive self-affirmations. Or you may hear background sounds such as the TV or family conversations. Take this time to breathe in the positive compliments you can grant yourself. Inhale any pleasant scents around you. You may smell your perfume or cologne, or perhaps you may light a candle to scent the room. Savor your moment by tasting lipstick or lip balm that you have applied to your lips. Complete this daily mindful task by choosing to feel beautiful.

Bathing in a bathtub can be your mindful moment of your day. **Bathe mindfully**. Take a look around your bathroom. What colors do you see? Consider where your bathtub is situated in your bathroom. What color is your bathtub? Do you have candles placed alongside your tub? Listen mindfully to the sound of the water pouring from the faucet, filling the bathtub. Bubbles may be starting to form. Inhale the fresh, clean scent of your body wash. Is it an outdoorsy scent? A fruity scent? You can almost taste the scent of the soap. Bubbles may even accidentally get in your mouth. As you are submerged in the warm water, remind yourself to feel the warmth. The warmer our body, the more relaxed we become. Remember to bathe mindfully.

How many times a day do you blow your nose? Once? Many? **Blow your nose mindfully**. Observe what you choose to blow your nose into. It is typically a tissue. Notice how you fold the tissue. In half? Quarters? Not at all? Hear the sound you make while blowing your nose. Do you blow your nose loudly? Or do you barely make a sound? As you blow into your tissue, perhaps you get a whiff of the tissue scent. You might even taste the perfumes used to scent the tissue or your very own body fluids. Feel the softness of the tissue as it touches your nose. Perhaps you felt a sneeze coming on prior to blowing your nose. Enjoy the satisfying moment of blowing your nose mindfully.

Brush your teeth mindfully. What are you thinking about when you brush your teeth? As you brush, look in the mirror. What do you see? Focus on the motion of the toothbrush. Feel the texture of the toothpaste foam in your mouth. Listen to the sound of the toothbrush as it brushes against your teeth. At this time, take a moment to taste the flavor of your toothpaste. Do you taste spearmint or peppermint? Cinnamon perhaps? Be mindful of the water temperature while rinsing your mouth. Do you rinse with warm, cool, or cold water? When you brush your teeth, you help remove food and plaque. Brushing your teeth mindfully gives you a moment to rest your brain and establish a positive mindset to start or end your day.

Caring for your pet mindfully can be incorporated into your daily life tasks. Utilizing your senses, look around the environment. Notice where the eating area may be situated or your pet's sleeping/shelter area is placed. Listen to the sounds your pet projects. Ask yourself if they are high- or low-pitched tones? For example, a bird whistle or a dog bark. Typically, these sounds indicate your pet's needs. Now, let's direct ourselves to care for our pet by incorporating our sense of smell. Taking a whiff of our pet may indicate they need a bath. Smelling the environment may also indicate your pet's bathroom or living area may need to be cleaned. Caring for your pet mindfully through taste may be a little challenging—although many people actually do taste their pet's food or give their pet human food. This could be fun if you make homemade meals for your pet. At last, feel your pet. Feeling your pet typically results in an increase of endorphins, oxytocin, and dopamine in the body, which is associated with positive feelings. Mindfully enjoy your relationship with your pet!

Do you like to clean? Whether your answer is yes or no, **clean mindfully**. Look around and assess what needs to be cleaned. Is it a small or large area? Will you begin cleaning from top to bottom, or perhaps left to right, or vice versa? Listen to the amplified sounds being emitted either by your manual cleaning or by your vacuum or similar device. Do the mirrors sound squeaky as you clean them with glass cleaner? Do you hear the noise from the vacuum? Does your broom make a sound as it sweeps the floor? Smell the clean scent from your cleaning solutions. Do you detect the scent of pine or lemon? The scent may be so strong that you can almost taste it. Embrace the cleansed feeling of a polished area, knowing it was cleaned mindfully.

While engaging in conversation, remember to **converse mindfully**. Look and make eye contact with the other person or people. Do you notice any unique facial features? Do they make any distinctive facial expressions? Actively listen to the tones of voice. Can you catch any noticeable vocal inflections? Is the other person a boisterous or a subdued conversationalist? Now, focus on their personal scent. Do you smell their perfume or cologne? By chance, do you detect a laundry detergent aroma from their clothes permeating the air? Savor the flavorful dialogue and taste the seasoning of emotions. Converse mindfully, embracing the warmth of the reciprocated chat.

Since cooking is typically a daily task, why not **cook mindfully**? This is a perfect time for all your senses to be heightened. Visually, in front of you is an array of colors from your different food groups. Proteins may give off shades of whites, pinks, and reds, while vegetables may give off shades of greens, yellows, and oranges. As you are prepping your food, listen to the different sounds. Do you hear a knife dicing on your chopping block? Is there sizzling going on in your sauté pan? Perhaps the best sense to be heightened while you cook mindfully is that of smell. Inhale all the aromas. What are you smelling? Mild or strong scents? Or maybe you think your sense of taste is the best sense to be heightened. Do you taste salty flavors? Do you taste sweetness? Tasting your delicious meal mindfully can warm your body, resulting in a pleasurable experience.

Whether you do one load or five loads of laundry a week, **do your laundry mindfully**. As you separate the darks from the lights, you are left with two piles of laundry in your visual field. How many different colors of clothing do you see? Do you notice shades of clothing in a particular color? While transferring the clothes to the washing machine, mindfully feel the fabrics. Do you feel soft cotton or silky synthetics? Get a whiff of the fresh laundry detergent as it pours into the washing machine. As you turn on the washing machine, hear the clicking sounds as you turn the dials to the proper settings. As you move the wet clothes to the dryer, feel the dampness in your arms. Once the dryer is turned on, bring your attention to the tumbling hum. As you empty the dryer, feel the warmth from the dry laundry. At this point, you can almost taste the flavor of the detergent. Do your laundry mindfully from now on for a richer experience.

Bring your beverage to your lips, and **drink mindfully**. Whether it's water, a carbonated drink, juice, tea, or coffee, be aware of your mindful moment. Take a look around. What do you see? Where are you enjoying your drink? Take note of any sounds you may be hearing while drinking mindfully—your own sipping or swallowing, or your own hmmm sounds of pleasure. Inhale the aroma of your beverage; smell the cleanliness of the water, the sweetness from the sugars, the lemon in the tea, or the roasted flavor of the coffee. Taste the liquid in your mouth. Is it a flat taste or a carbonated taste? If carbonated, feel the bubbles bursting on your tongue. Are you drinking a hot or cold beverage? Feel the liquid of your drink as you sip, swallow, or guzzle. Take pleasure in drinking mindfully.

How often do you drive to your destination without remembering the drive? **Drive mindfully**. While driving, observe the road. Be aware of landmarks you may pass, the variation in the landscape along the way, and so on. Take a look at your hands on the steering wheel. As you cruise down the street, listen to the song on the radio. There may be conversations you hear from others in the car. Or you may be driving in silence. Become familiar with your vehicle's scent. Is it the smell of a new car? The aroma of air freshener? The smell of a snack in the car? During your drive, feel the fresh air from the open windows, the cool blast from the air-conditioner, or the warmth from the heater. To stay present on your drive, remember to incorporate all your senses. This can help alleviate any anxiety you may have when driving to an unfamiliar destination.

When you are styling your hair, use your hairdryer to **dry your hair mindfully**. Take your moment to focus on your hair. Notice your hair color. Do you have long or short hair? How is your hair styled? While you mindfully blow-dry your hair, listen to the white noise. Is the blow-dryer on high or low speed? Take a whiff of your freshly shampooed hair. Do you smell any hair products? Sometimes you can even taste the chemical particles floating in the air. Take this time to feel the brush in your hand as you blow-dry your hair mindfully. Embrace the warmth from the dryer as it warms your scalp and body. Handle your newly styled hair mindfully, feeling beautiful.

As you indulge in your breakfast, lunch, dinner, or snack, **eat mindfully**. Be aware of your senses. What is in your visual field? Are you eating at home or in a restaurant? What sounds do you hear while eating mindfully? Can you hear your own chewing resonating in your ears? Perhaps you hear the sound from the silverware touching your teeth? What do you smell? The food, of course! Do you smell strong or mild aromas? Is it a recognizable scent? Do you like the smell? Now, taste the food. Are your taste buds experiencing sweet, salty, sour, or bitter? What is the texture and consistency of your food? Feel the temperature of the food in your mouth. Enjoy the refreshing cold trickling through your body or the hot temperature relaxing your soul. Complete your mindful eating moment by feeling fulfilled while feasting.

How many times a day do you catch yourself on social media? The next time you log on, whether it is Facebook, Instagram, Twitter, Snapchat, or TikTok, **engage in social media mindfully**. Take a moment to immerse yourself in the newsfeed. Reading the posts or scrolling through the images stimulates your visual sense. You may start to connect with words or photos. While scanning the bulletins, hear your own inner voice. Listen to your own comments. Are they positive or negative? In doing so, ask yourself, "What kind of smell fills my space?" Depending on if your thoughts are positive or negative, this may result in identifying a pleasant or unpleasant scent around you. Be cognizant of the taste social media leaves in your mouth. Are you left with a sweet or sour taste? In engaging with your social media mindfully, you can fill your mind and body with warm, positive thoughts, resulting in a pleasant experience. It is all up to you.

Eat dessert and celebrate yourself daily. All you need is just one bite. **Enjoy your dessert mindfully**. A dessert can provide a delicious visual to your eyes. Is it cake? Cookie? Candy? Fruit? What color is your treat? While getting ready to indulge in your mindful moment, listen to the sounds you make while preparing to eat your dessert. Notice the sound of your fork as it enters your mouth. Listen to yourself chewing and swallowing. During your decadent moment, you can smell the sweetness as you taste the delectable, satisfying flavor. Eating your dessert mindfully allows you to honor and reward yourself, which may result in the feeling of higher self-esteem and self-empowerment.

Getting your hair done is all about you, so **enjoy your haircut mindfully**. Begin by being present as you walk into the salon. Take a look around at the place. After check-in, it is typically time for the shampoo experience. With your head tilted back in the sink, listen to the water wet your hair. You can smell the scent of the shampoo and relax as the warm water rinses through your hair. Then comes the mindful haircut experience itself. Get a whiff of the hair products. Listen to the scissors or razor clip your hair. Feel the warm air from the blow-dryer. The end result will be a taste of beautiful confidence as you exit the salon having had a mindful haircut experience.

Where do you exercise? Whether it is indoors or outdoors, **exercise mindfully**. Be mindful of your exercise territory. Look to see what is in your visual field. Are you looking in a mirror? Are you in nature? Be observant of your surroundings. What are some of the sounds you may be encountering? If exercising in a gym, you may hear the weights clanging together or the thump of a weight hitting the floor. If exercising in nature, you may hear birds chirping or airplanes flying overhead. When exercising mindfully outdoors, you may come across aromas of flowers blooming or air impurities. If in a gym, you may smell the odor exuded by the exercise mats. While exercising, you may experience the taste of salty sweat dripping off your face and entering your mouth. Exercising mindfully can result in a sensation of bodily burn. It can also result in warmth and satisfaction.

Feed your pets mindfully. This is your time to be in the moment with this daily task. Notice where you feed your pet(s). Are you inside or outside? Observe the type of pet food. Is it dry or moist? Listen to the sound of the dry pet food as it pours from the bag. Or do you hear the sound from the can opener opening the can of pet food? What are you smelling as you feed your pet(s) mindfully? Typically, as soon as either the bag or can of pet food opens, you can smell it. For some, it is a tolerable aroma and for others, not so much. You can almost predict the taste of the pet food based on its smell. Feeding your pet mindfully results in a warm feeling within yourself, knowing you cared for your pet consciously.

Do you floss daily? It may be an annoying task for you, but if you **floss mindfully**, it can be a satisfying experience. Where do you floss your teeth? Are you in a bathroom? Do you floss in your car? Notice what is in your visual field and detect the floss dispenser. Mindfully holding the floss, feel the string wrap around your fingers. Tune in to the snap sound of the floss as it is torn off the dispenser. Listen to the pop sound you hear as the floss fits between your teeth. As you continue to floss mindfully, you may even get a whiff of the scent of your mouth. Perhaps you begin to taste your own breath. Or maybe you can taste the flavor of fresh mint from the dental floss. Finish flossing mindfully with the comforting feeling of self-care.

Getting your nails done is your time for some self-care. **Get a manicure mindfully**. Ask yourself, "What is in my visual field?" Are you at a nail or hair salon? In someone's home? Take a look around and notice the space in which you are getting pampered. Now, listen to the sounds you hear. Is it the voice of your manicurist? Other conversations? Or just maybe your own inner voice? Usually, when getting a manicure, you can smell the fumes from the nail products in the air. Typically, if you are in a nail salon, you are offered water. Be mindful while you sip your water. Relax as you soak your hands in the bowl of water, feeling the warmth. The result of a mindful manicure is feeling beautiful with a visual of freshly polished nails.

While you engage in your daily task of walking to pick up your mail, remember to **get your mail mindfully**. Recognize the path on which you stroll to your mailbox. Pinpoint the location of your mailbox. Observe the size, shape, and color of your mailbox. What sounds to do hear while you get your mail mindfully? Possibly the jingling of keys as you insert the key into the mailbox? Maybe the echo or squeak from opening and closing a metal mailbox? Take this mindful moment to inhale the oxygen around you. If your mailbox is inside, identify any aromas. Feel the temperature from the air-conditioner or perhaps from the heater. If you must venture outside for your mail, inhale the fresh air. Feel the climate. Warm sunrays? Cold, windy rain? Practice getting mail mindfully by walking back to your destination with your mail, knowing you did so in a tasteful manner.

For some, grocery shopping can create sensory overload, so **grocery shop mindfully**. Start by asking yourself what is in your visual field. Walking down the grocery aisle, observe the colorful cans stacked and organized fashion. You may notice what other shoppers have in their shopping carts. You might be looking for the best produce. All the while, listen to what you hear around you. Conversations? Piped-in store music? Announcements on the loudspeaker? Become aware of your olfactory sense and inhale. You may smell freshly baked bread from the bakery. How about the aroma of recently popped popcorn in the deli section? While grocery shopping mindfully, you may be tasting the food samples. Be mindful of the flavors and textures that enter your mouth. The idea is to finish your grocery shopping feeling satisfied in your present moment in which you incorporated all your senses.

Hugging releases oxytocin—the love hormone. **Hug someone mindfully**. As you go to give a hug, look at the other person. Observe their stature. Will you be reaching high or low to hug them? Will you put your arms around their neck, back, or waist? What kind of embrace will this be? An intimate one? A polite one-way or buddy hug? Pay attention to the tones and inflections of the voice of the person approaching you. Be aware of the sounds around you as you embrace. Whether you hold each other for a brief mindful moment or linger a little longer, mindfully get a whiff of the scent around you. Do you smell perfume, cologne, or a natural body aroma? At this point, you can almost taste the connection resulting from your mindful hug. While hugging mindfully, you feel the embrace of arms around you and feel the affection. This is your mindful moment to be present while giving and receiving a hug.

Do you iron your clothes? If so, **iron mindfully**. Where do you find yourself ironing garments? Take a look around and notice where the iron is placed in the room. Is it on an ironing board? Is it near a washer and dryer? Perhaps in front of a TV? As you begin to iron mindfully, tune in to the sounds from the iron. Do you hear the steam spraying onto the fabric? While ironing, you may get a whiff of laundry detergent or other scents as the cloth becomes hot. Be mindful of those aromas. When you lift the iron up, notice the heaviness. You may feel the water spray or the steam condensing on your hands from the iron. Experience the warmth you sense from the fabric as you iron mindfully. Savor the task as you produce a fresh, crisply ironed garment, knowing you ironed it mindfully.

When you kiss your significant other, **kiss mindfully**. Connect with that person through your senses. Engage eye to eye. Gaze at their facial features. Notice physical traits. As you kiss mindfully, is it a long passionate kiss or a short peck? Either way, listen to your lips pressing on each other's. During your moment, take a whiff to smell your significant other's scent. Do you smell perfume or cologne? The aroma of their soap or the scent of their body? Feel your lips against theirs. Is it a dry or wet kiss? Are your lips smooth or chapped? When you kiss mindfully, you can taste the love you have for each other.

Do you **laugh mindfully**? Notice in your visual field who or what is around you and where you are laughing. Are you laughing by yourself or with someone? Are you chuckling at a live or inanimate object? Is your laughing environment inside or outside? Next, listen intently to the inflection from your laugh. Is the sound of your laugh high-pitched or soft? Do you tend to linger your chuckle or burst your cackle? Now, detect any odors circling you. While laughing mindfully, do you like or dislike the smell? Is the aroma new or familiar to you? Pay attention to your muscles while you laugh mindfully. Feel your face, jaw, and throat muscles flex. In addition, feel the muscles in your abdomen expand and contract. Practice laughing mindfully as often as possible utilizing all your senses.

Make love mindfully. Senses are already heightened during lovemaking, so let yourself be mindful in the moment. Observe your partner. Focus on their facial features and their physical appearance. What do you see that attracts you to your partner? Turn your attention now to the sounds of passion. Do you hear heavy breathing? Perhaps you are listening to words of endearment from your significant other. Tune in to the harmony when both bodies connect as one. When making love mindfully, inhale each other's body scents. Do you and your lover have your own unique smell? Do you smell perfume or cologne? To make love mindfully, taste the passion. Devour each other. Savor the kisses. Feel the warmth as you embrace each other. Embrace the love-making experience and remember to incorporate all your senses.

Think about how often you are on the phone each day. **Make phone calls mindfully**. Where do you find yourself talking on the phone? Are you inside or outside? Are you holding the phone, using the speakerphone feature, or using earbuds? Listen intently to the voice on the other end—the other person's tone and inflections as they speak to you. Inhale the connection between the two of you. While exhaling, recognize the dynamic of the relationship. This may result in either an unpleasant or a pleasant taste in your mouth. End the phone call with a satisfying feeling, knowing you were present with the person on the other end.

When you wake up in the morning, a great way to start your day is to **make your bed mindfully**. Look at your unmade bed. Are the sheets wrinkled? What does the blanket look like? Is it messy or neat? As you begin making your bed mindfully, hear the sound the blanket makes while flipping it into place. Feel the quick movement of warm air as you adjust the blanket. Your nose will get a whiff of your personal space. Perhaps you smell the scent from your laundry detergent or linen spray. Feel the softness as you glide your hands to flatten out any wrinkles. The visual of a mindfully made bed starts off your day with a positive taste in your mouth.

What is your reading material of choice? A book? An e-reader? The internet? Whatever your tool, **read mindfully**. Visually connect to your reading material. Are you looking at paper literature or at a screen? Notice the font style and any visual graphics. What are you hearing at this time? The sound of turning pages? The sound of your mouse scrolling down your screen? Perhaps you hear your inner voice as you read to yourself. When you read a book mindfully, you can often smell the paper-bound pages. Holding the reading material in your hands, you can feel the texture of the book or magazine. If reading on a screen, you can feel its smooth surface. While reading mindfully, you can feel the words nourishing your brain.

If you typically shave on a regular basis, as many people do, why not **shave mindfully**? Shaving usually happens in a shower, in a bathtub, or in front of the bathroom sink. This is your mindful moment to be present to your daily task. Connect to your senses. What sort of sounds do you hear while shaving? Perhaps it is the buzz from an electric shaver or the sound of running water? Smell the scent from the soap or shaving cream. Feel the lather on your skin as you gently shave your legs, underarms, bikini area, or face. When men shave their mustache or beard, they may even accidentally taste the shaving cream. Feel the warm water rinse off the foam. The end result is smooth skin and the knowledge that a daily task was performed while being mindful of the present moment.

It does not matter if you shower in the morning or at night or how many showers you take a day. What matters is that you **shower mindfully**. Once in the shower, this is your mindful moment to be in your moment. Just be still. Take a look around. Are you seeing a tile pattern on the shower walls? Are you behind a shower curtain with a particular color or theme? Perhaps you are enclosed in a glass shower. What are you hearing? Usually, you will hear the stream of water as it hits your body. Maybe you hear music or TV in the background. Are you perhaps listening to your own thoughts? As you shower mindfully, inhale the scent of your body wash. The smell of cleanliness emerges as you lather the soap. You may even accidentally taste the soap as it rinses off your face. Feel the soothing water wash away your suds. The warmer the water and higher your body temperature in the shower, the more relaxed you will feel. End your shower knowing you incorporated all your senses. Ahhh!

If you live in a cold-weather climate, **sit in front of a fire mindfully**. As you relax in front of a fireplace or campfire, fix your eyes on the flames. Focus on the glowing yellows and oranges. The crackling sound from the burning wood logs fills your ears. Smell the cedar as the fire flickers and the scent consumes the air. Sitting in front of a fire, you can almost taste the warmth you feel from the flames. The warmth from the fire raises your body temperature. This results in a calmer and more relaxed feeling. Another option may be to gaze at a candle mindfully. It does not matter the size of the flames but the experience.

Wherever you go, you often have to sit, so why not **sit mindfully**? Visually take in your surroundings. Notice where you are sitting. Are you on a chair? Inside or outside? Alone? With others? Listen closely to what you are hearing while sitting mindfully. Your own thoughts? Listening to others? Background music? Get a good sense of the smell of your sitting place. What aroma are you breathing in? Is it a familiar or new smell? While sitting mindfully, you may also be tasting something. Perhaps a beverage or a snack, or perhaps you've sat down to eat a meal. Be mindful of what you are tasting while you sit. Feel the surface of your seat against your buttocks. Is what you are sitting on hard or soft? Sitting mindfully results in being present with oneself, which results in a calmer state. Remember to sit mindfully and enjoy your moment.

How will you know if you **sleep mindfully**? Start off by observing your own sleeping space. Where is your bed located in the room? Look at your blanket, sheet, and pillow(s). What is the color(s) of your blanket, sheets? Perhaps there is a pattern on the pillowcase? As you slip under the sheet or blanket, listen to the sound of the fabric sliding against your body. You may hear the sound from your TV, your music, or calming chimes as part of your mindful sleeping routine. Incorporate what you smell. Take a whiff of your sheets, your pillow, and your blanket. Do you smell the aroma from your laundry detergent? Perhaps you smell your own body scent. Ask yourself, "What am I tasting as I sleep mindfully?" Typically, after brushing your teeth before bed, you will taste your own fresh, minty breath. Complete your mindful sleep by feeling your feet rub the softness of the sheets. Feel the warmth radiate from under your covers. Embrace your daily mindful moment of sleeping and sleep peacefully.

Catch yourself smiling throughout the day! To **smile mindfully**, begin by looking around. What in your field of vision are you smiling about? A person, place, or thing? Do certain colors in your visual field make you smile? Observe the environment you are smiling mindfully in and relish the moment. Tune in to the sounds you hear while smiling. Do you hear others' voices? Are you listening to music or hearing the TV? Maybe a quiet hum brings a smile to your face. Next, take a whiff of your surroundings. Inhale through your nose and exhale through your mouth. Identify any familiar and unfamiliar scents. The olfactory sense can elicit a mindful smile. Last, get a good taste of smiling. Smiling is a universal gesture. It suggests to others that you are approachable and kind. When you smile, feel your facial muscles flexing. Smiling increases your happy hormones, or endorphins. When you smile mindfully, your brain feels happier.

Instead of aimlessly reaching for snacks throughout the day, **snack mindfully**. How often do you snack daily? Whether your snacks are healthy foods or junk foods, incorporate all your senses while snacking. Observe your snack visually. Is it a natural food with no packaging? Does your snack come in a box or bag? What color is your snack? Listen carefully to the sound your snack makes while enjoying your mindful moment. Do you hear a crunchy or perhaps a chewy sound? Possibly you'll hear no sound at all while enjoying your snack. Be aware of the aroma from your snack as it fills your nose with deliciousness. As you hold your snack in your hand, feel the texture. Is your snack smooth or rough? The best part of snacking mindfully is tasting. As you taste, identify the flavor and the temperature of the food. Do you taste sweet or salty? Is your snack cold or hot? It doesn't matter what your snack is as long as you snack mindfully.

We use our money on something every day, so why not **spend mindfully**? Whether it is how much to spend for the day or the week, keep in mind how you are budgeting your funds. When you disburse your earnings, are you using cash or credit/debit cards? Open your wallet and look at your form of money. Do you see the green of the cash, the shine of coins, or perhaps the colors from credit or debit cards? Now, listen to the sound of the paper money as you separate your bills. Hear the coins jingle in your hand. Pay attention to the noise from the swipe of the flexible cards. As you spend mindfully, inhale the air around you. Think about if the aroma you're smelling is familiar or unfamiliar to you. As you are being mindful of your financial contributions, be aware of what taste it leaves in your mouth. Is it a good or bad one? Be present while paying and feel the texture of the bills, the smooth coins, or the plastic from the credit or debit card. Finish your transaction knowing you spent mindfully, fully present in your moment.

Learn how to **stretch mindfully**. Where do you find yourself stretching your body? In your bed? On your yoga mat? Whatever the environment, take your mindful moment to notice what is in your visual space. Do you see your bed linens, your office desk, or perhaps others on yoga mats? Take your mindful moment while stretching to listen to the surrounding sounds. What do you hear? TV? Conversations? Quiet? Breathe in through your nose, recognizing any familiar scents. Exhale through your mouth. Ahhhh! Feel your muscles elongating, activating your parasympathetic nervous system to increase blood flow. No wonder stretching feels so good! Stretching mindfully releases endorphins, which enhance mood, resulting in a positive taste in your mouth for the rest of your day.

Do you **take out the trash mindfully**? Taking out the trash does not have to be a chore. Instead, make it your mindful moment! Typically, we take garbage outside to the curb or to a garbage chute. If you are walking outside to deposit your trash, look up at the sky. What color do you see? Or are you walking inside down a hallway? What do you see as you walk to your garbage chute? Now listen to your surroundings. Do you hear birds chirping? Do you hear the sounds from vehicles? Maybe you hear quiet from indoor hallways. Take a mindful moment to focus on your olfactory sense. Inhale the air. What do you smell? The odor from the trash, perhaps? The fresh, clean air? Unless you are chewing something, there isn't much to taste while taking out the trash mindfully, but you can taste the success of knowing that taking out your trash was a mundane experience made mindful.

You have hundreds of thoughts throughout the day, so why not make them meaningful? **Think mindfully**. Ask yourself, "Where am I in my mindful thought?" Look around. Focus on your surroundings. Do you find yourself inside or outside? What are you thinking about? Listen to your own ideas; hear your inner voice, tone, and inflections. Pay attention to your beliefs. Allow your present thought to be aware of the odors that surround you. Identify what you are smelling while you are thinking mindfully. Your impressions can leave a variety of tastes in your mouth. Positive thoughts will result in a pleasant taste. Finish your mindful thinking with a sense of feeling present in your moment.

Tidy up mindfully. Let's put things away in a mindful manner. First, look around your environment. Where are you? What room are you in? Or perhaps you are cleaning up an outdoor space. Assess the items in your visual field that need to be put away. Are you looking at piles of papers? Are you seeing lots of toys? Pick up on any sounds you may be hearing. Do you hear the TV? The vacuum running? The dishwasher going? Inhale the air around you and identify any aromas. Do you smell a candle burning? Maybe cleaning supplies? While holding the items you mindfully intend to tidy up, feel the different textures and temperatures in your hands. Are you putting away soft clothes? Maybe you are putting away frozen groceries. Last, savor the area you just straightened out. Tidying up mindfully should not be a chore but a sensory experience. Have fun!

We all use the bathroom, but do we **use the bathroom mindfully**? Take your moment to consider your lavatory environment. Are you in your home powder room? A public restroom? Are you in a familiar or unfamiliar surrounding? Listen to what is going on around you. Is it quiet? Do you hear others? Perhaps you are paying attention to piped-in music. The range of odors you experience while using the bathroom can be extreme—whether you are smelling your own bathroom experience or someone else's. Perhaps you detect the pleasant aromatic aroma that is emitted into the air by your own atomizer or perhaps the inescapable public restroom scent. Finishing up with your mindful bathroom experience, you typically wash your hands. At this time, you can almost taste the scent of the soap as you cleanse. The end result of going to the bathroom mindfully is a sense of relief.

How many hours a day are you on your computer? **Use your computer mindfully**. As you focus on the screen, notice the colors. Look at the different font styles and the layout of your apps, perhaps. Recognize where your toolbar is located or the pop-ups that may appear on your screen. While typing, feel the smooth keys under your fingertips. What do you hear? The tapping of your keystrokes? Infomercials or background music? Notification alert sounds? What do you smell while you are on your computer? Your office scent? House aroma? Do you sip a drink or munch on a snack while you are at your computer? When you use your computer mindfully, acknowledge the sweet taste of accomplishment.

Good morning, sunshine! It's time to **wake up mindfully**. As your eyes open, look around and observe where your bed is positioned in the room. Are you facing a window? A TV? A wall? What color is the room painted? What other furniture is in your space? This is your mindful moment while waking up in the morning or from an afternoon nap to listen. Are birds chirping? Do you hear the sound of an alarm clock? Is there music or a TV on? Or maybe you just hear the sound of stillness. Inhale the scent of your blanket, your sheets, and your pillow. Recognize your own familiar scent. Feel the warmth from your blankets warming your body. When you wake up mindfully, you can taste the positive day ahead of you.

Most of us walk every day, so why not **walk mindfully**? This is a perfect moment to look around and be present with your surroundings. Where are you walking to or from? What are you observing on your mindful walk? Trees? Buildings? People? Be in tune with the sounds around you. Do you hear the rustling of leaves in the wind? Birds chirping? Automobile sounds? Inhale the air all around you. What are you smelling? Flowers blooming? A fireplace burning? Air pollutants? As you walk mindfully, you can almost taste the rejuvenation that comes from self-care. Finish up your mindful walk by feeling the outside temperature. Are the sun's rays warming your body? Is the moonlit-night air cooling you off? It is known that mindful walking has the benefit of promoting a healthy quality of life. Mindful walking takes practice so do it as often as possible. Complete your walk, knowing you walked mindfully in your moment.

Do you like to wash dishes? Probably not, but if you have to, **wash dishes mindfully**. You can make this task as pleasant as possible by utilizing your senses. Assess the situation. Take a good look at the sink full of dishes and decide how you will tackle washing. Are you first looking to find all the silverware to clean, or will you begin by scrubbing the pots and pans? As you wash the dishes, listen to the sound of the water. Do you hear other sounds? TV? Conversations? Typically, you can smell the scent of the dish soap as you mindfully wash the utensils and dishes. Do you smell the aroma of lemons, or is it a floral scent? Allow the hot water to warm your skin as you hold the sponge in your hand. Feel the dish soap lather in your hands. While rinsing, continue to experience the feeling of warm water on your skin. Taste the satisfaction of washing the dishes mindfully, resulting in a clean and empty sink.

Wash your hands mindfully for a pleasurable experience. Incorporate all your senses in your moment of hand washing. Begin by observing where you are stationed while you are washing your hands. Notice the type of faucet, the shape of the sink perhaps, and where the soap may be located. Then listen to the water streaming from the tap. Hear your hands cleaning each other while lathering them with soap. Take your mindful moment of hand washing to smell the aroma of the soapsuds. You can almost taste the cleanliness of your hands. Finish your mindful hand washing experience by feeling the warm water cleanse away the germs and welcoming the sensation of freshly cleansed hands. Always remember this takeaway—the warmer our body, the more relaxed we are. Wash your hands with warm water!

Whether you watch good old-fashioned cable TV, Netflix, Hulu, or Amazon Prime, the idea is to **watch shows mindfully**. What do you watch your shows on? Is it a TV? A computer? Possibly a tablet? Take a look at your screen. How big is it? Where is it situated in the room? Look at the visual images on your screen. Be mindful of your auditory sense. Connect with the voices from your show. Listen to the background music from your show. Can you identify any sound effects? While watching your show mindfully, become aware of any aromas in the air. Are they familiar or unfamiliar smells to you? Some of us eat our meal or snack while watching our show. If you do this, be aware of what you are eating—the taste, the texture, and so on. This mindful experience results in even more pleasure and joy while watching your show.

Wherever you happen to be when it is raining, take a moment to **watch the rain mindfully**. Are you indoors or outdoors as you observe the rain? Look to see what direction the rain is falling. Is it a heavy or light rain? Be mindful of the pitter-patter of the rain as it lands. The noise of thunder and bright flashes of lightning may accompany the rain. Inhale and smell the familiar scent of rainfall, that pleasant earthy smell as the droplets hit the soil. You can almost taste the rain from the aroma in the air. You may even open your mouth and taste the rainwater. While watching the rain mindfully, you may feel the humidity or coolness from the air. Remember to watch rain mindfully. Watching rain can be compared to listening to pink noise, which has the ability to reduce brainwaves. This outcome increases alpha brain waves, which can result in a calmer state of mind. Stop and watch the rain!

When you are working, **work mindfully**. While sitting at your desk either at your place of employment or at home, take note of where your workspace is located. Where is your desk situated? What is in your visual field? Listen to the familiar and not-so-familiar sounds around you. Do you hear the air-conditioner click on and off? Coworkers' voices? The sound of your keyboard as you type? Notice any aromas. The smell of coffee? The scent of air freshener? Someone's perfume? Embrace your tasks, aware of what you are actually feeling with your hands. Maybe you work with paper or perhaps a metal machine. Feel the texture of what you work with in your hands. Recognize what you are tasting. At times, we eat while working. If you are not eating, you may encounter a metallic taste in your mouth from red blood cells. Practice working mindfully by applying focus and awareness with your senses. Feel the sense of productivity and the taste of success it leaves in your mouth.

Who writes these days? Whether it is a list, a journal or a doodle, **write mindfully**. Whether you write with a pen, pencil, or magic marker, do it mindfully. Look at your writing utensil. What is the ink color? Or are you using a traditional yellow #2 pencil? Observe how you hold your writing implement. Can you hear your writing tool marking the paper? Be aware of your hand motion as it glides along the smooth surface. The writing apparatus may emit an odor, such as with a magic marker. Take note of the scent. If you hold the pencil to your nose, you may smell the cedar. You can almost imagine what these smells would taste like. Writing mindfully is a rewarding sensory experience.

Acknowledgments

To my husband, **Brett**, who supports and nourishes my soul. Together since we were fifteen years old, we set our goals and made our dreams come true. Thank you for inspiring me daily and loving me like no other. I adore you! Together forever.

To my daughters, **Sydney** and **Kennedy**, whom I admire for their strong, empathetic, passionate natures. You both are determined, committed, patient individuals who make me so very proud. Thank you for all the support and laughter. I love you both more.

To my mom, **Merryl** (aka **Grandi**). Thank you for always believing in me, encouraging me, and loving me. I admire your strength, resilience, and humor. I only hope to be half the mother you are to me.

To my dad, **Stephen**, and my brother, **Keith**, who have passed away. I thank them for being the best father and brother they could for me. Keith, I may not have granted your wish to attain a doctorate, but I became an author instead!

To my mother-in-law, **Gayle**. I thank you for all your love and support. You always believe in me, and I am grateful you are one of my biggest fans. Blessed to call you my "second" mom.

To my son-in-law, **Alan**. Thank you for your patience, kindness and countless hours of computer knowledge. All your time and efforts are deeply appreciated. Love you dearly.

To my **family** and **friends**. Thank you for believing in me and supporting my book journey. I especially want to thank my sister-in-law and exceptional friend, **Sheila**, for designing Live Mindfully 52 Ways to bring my book to life! For all your words of affirmation and involvement in this book process.

To the women who inspired me to write a book. I thank **Beth**, **Monique**, **Tana**, **Kimi**, **Diana** and **Melissa**. Thank you for your encouragement and guidance.

To my **clients** who have thanked me for helping them with my mindful therapeutic practices. I thank you for sharing your journey to success with me.

To The Book Couple, **Carol** and **Gary**. Thank you for making my book a reality.

To my **readers**, Thank you for your interest in Live Mindfully 52 Ways.

I wish us all a mindful day!

Let's Stay Connected!

"Thank you for reading Live Mindfully 52 Ways! If you found inspiration in these pages, I'd love to hear your thoughts. Your review not only helps me but also guides other readers on their mindfulness journey. Sharing just a few words makes a big difference!"

Here's where to connect:

- Facebook @ Live Mindfully 52 Ways
- Instragram @ livemindfully52ways
- TikTok @ livemindfully52ways
- FrancineMarksWeinstein.com
- FrancineMarksWeinstein@gmail.com